TIME TO HEAL

TIME TO HEAL

ART & WORDS BY
MAYA GONZALEZ

I dedicate this book to the
healing force within all that
is and to all humans.
It's time to evolve.
—MG

Published by Reflection Press,
San Francisco, CA since 2009

ISBN 978-1-945289-28-6
Book Design & Production by Matthew S.G.

Reflection Press is a POC, queer, and trans owned independent publisher of radical and revolutionary children's books and works that expand cultural and spiritual awareness. Rooted in holistic, nature-based, and anti-oppression frameworks, our materials support a strong sense of individuality along with a community model of real inclusion.
Visit us at **www.reflectionpress.com** and **www.genderwheel.com**

For permissions, bulk orders, or if you receive a misprinted book, please contact us at info@reflectionpress.com

heal everything everything heals

HEALING CONTENTS

TIME TO HEAL

WELCOME

Healing is high on my mind right now. One, because I am dealing with breast cancer. And two, because we are in huge political flux. It's bound to be a challenging era of transformation for many of us. So, it's not just personal. Profound healing is also needed nationally and globally. Everything needs healing. How to begin?

I have healed. And I will heal again. I have had the kinds of healings that are unexpected, against all odds. The kind people call miracles. I have learned many things in my living and almost dying.

Since death has been with me since I was young, I have used my creativity to help me survive, understand myself and the world around me and source deep personal power. I have learned up front that the creative force that flows through all things flows powerfully through us and we can use it to heal, to know, to transcend and integrate.

Let me say first, this is a long dance. This is not something we're going to breeze through and be done. This is a time of reckoning. Whether it's purely personal or even wholly political, we must come face to face with illusion, our histories and lessons and much more. There will be challenging feelings and change that must occur. We will think we know what we're doing and what's going on only to find out we were misled either by ourselves or others. Our greatest strength will be how fluid and flexible we can stay. But strong. But gentle. It's a delicate balance. It's a healing dance. This planner is designed to help us focus as we go.

THE FLOW OF TIME

The months and weeks are undated. You can pick it up at any time and begin. You can even drop in and out if necessary. There are 13 sections. This provides the possibility of 13 lunar cycles or using it beyond the 12-month year. The format is meant to support dropping into whatever flow works for you.

HEALING FORMAT

The planner is set up as a healing ritual. The backdrop of every page reads "everything heals" and "heal everything" over and over. Every time you write or look at the pages you are energizing the affirmation whether you are conscious of it or not. This reminds us that every act can heal us and at any moment we can drop into a larger healing flow. It is always there.

I specifically curated the art and stories to symbolize what I have gathered over the years that keeps me strong as I heal now. Much of the healing energy is nonverbal, embedded in the imagery. I often don't fully comprehend my work until years later.

My healing is your healing. Your healing is my healing. The planner is about the possibility of creating a constant healing frame of mind as a people.

TAKING ACTION

The most powerful place to begin is always within. Here we heal the depths and patterns of our lives, the core of our lesson. There is nothing that we do on the outside that does not begin within. Within lies true power.

However, this is not to say that we are not taking action on the outside. In fact, when we make ourselves strong on the inside it is easier, even more compelling, to take action on the outside. This is about making us stronger so that we can take action and dance this dance as long as possible until all people are free.

MY HEALINGS

I have had 3 brushes with death:

When I was 7, I had a serious head injury and was not expected to make it. I was in a coma for 3 days. When I did come out I was heavily medicated for 2 years to prevent seizures. A full recovery seemed unlikely, but hopefully I'd get by in life.

When I begged to be taken out of school because I couldn't stand the bullying, they took me off the meds instead. Much to everyone's surprise I scored at a high intelligence level on their placement tests and never had any seizures.

In 1995, through the negligence of a screen printer, I was poisoned with heavy metals. I managed without understanding what was going on until 2003 when my health took a huge dive. I was finally diagnosed after I had a vision of a rusting metal wall and asked to have my heavy metals tested. I found that I was off the chart for numerous metals. 9 Western doctors told me *"I should be dead"* and that they could do nothing for me. I was too weak. I worked with a spiritual healer instead and experienced a complete healing after 10+ years of being sick, 3 of which I was almost completely incapacitated.

In 2023, I was diagnosed with advanced breast cancer after thinking it was something else for over 2 years. I had chemo and targeted therapies. Just 3 months post chemo it started growing again. I am currently working with the same healer as with the heavy metals. There is always time to heal.

ABOUT THE SMALL PIECES OF ART

While disabled with heavy metals, I began using ink on vintage book pages because it was physically easiest. This reconnected me with my childhood love of line drawings and fountain pens. With my declining health my work got small and afterward it stayed small. Instead of large pieces, I now processed my experiences through these series on small bits of paper leftover from my children's book illustrations.

BVM (circa 2013 coffee/tea stains, ink and watercolor)

I was painting numerous small pieces I call the FridaJizo Series: a fusion of Frida as a healing symbol and the Japanese Jizo. Jizos are statues placed along the road that symbolize a guardian deity of children and travelers. Jizos are also known as the 'earth bearer' and predate Buddhist beliefs.

An old friend saw them and asked me if I would do what they called "BVM's" (blessed virgin Mary's) in the same style.

I exploded. I needed to make 13 of them to get them through my system. I remembered all the BVM statues I saw as a child, and I transformed each one.

Singing girl series (circa 2008 archival ink)

I had an entirely different life after I healed from the heavy metals. I was thrilled, but I also had to come to terms with the life I had lived. I often didn't have words. Only lines.

A series of singing girls came through wearing dresses from when I was very young. They had wild hair and sometimes fur growing for arms and legs. The singing was usually joyous, joining an ethereal chorus. The fur symbolized wild freedom and unbounded growth.

Deer hoods and spires (circa 2010 archival ink)

I created these during a time of intense transformation. I felt keenly aware of life shifting and enormous loss, but I seldom had words for what I was experiencing. There are other larger pieces related to these small ones where the characters have huge gowns and ghosts.

At one point, the deer transformed into spires of geometry and wild fur. I'd never seen anything like it before. But since then I have discovered the history of the Motanka, ancient dolls rooted in divine femme, rural traditions of Slavic countries. The dolls remind me of my GG who came from Poland. GG taught me to crochet when I was 4.

WRITING RITUAL

Take the time to do the full writing ritual for yourself.

I began at the top of a blank sheet of paper and wrote "*everything heals*" across the page. On the next line I wrote "*heal everything*" across the page. I repeated this down the entire length of the page. Back and forth. I played with each line's writing style, but mostly I paid attention to the words.

I was having an unusually hard time when I started, but by the time I finished I had more perspective and ease. I laughed. It worked!

'TIME TO HEAL' COVER IMAGE

The image on the cover is the last large piece I painted. It connects me with the time before I became a full-time parent and began to focus more on children's books and gender diversity instead of fine art. Although it took me years to stop thinking about painting, I love my current work. And I know one day I will paint like this again. The wonderful thing is that I currently live with a lot of my art. It makes me so happy.

I love working before dawn. It's an empty quiet that prepares me for the day and the world beyond. As I've navigated cancer and chemo, I've spent a lot of hours in the early morning not working but staring at this piece. It's positioned so that I'm right in front of it in the kitchen. If I look up, it's looking right at me.

In the fine art world, I am known for my imagery of big round breasts and bellies as an homage to bodies like mine. And hair. They always have hair. Sometimes hugely flowing symbolic hair. So, this piece stands out. All I remember from the time that I painted it is that this was a portrait of a powerful force of divinity flowing through.

After staring at it for months, I finally realized that this painting has been ME staring back at ME all along. Over a decade before I had cancer, I painted myself healing through it. Bald. Breast free. Divine flowers sprouting from spirit to heal my heart on the left side where the cancer has been. Everything vibrating in vibrant hot pinks, my favorite color as a kid. This is me. My largest, biggest, healing self.

This painting is a message through time to remind myself that I am spirit, and I will heal through this.

Life is art.

Living is healing.

EVERYTHING HEALS.

1.

LIFE IS RITUAL
Embracing divine femme power

I've always loved a good gown. The first time I put on my parent's wedding dress, I got so excited I ran down the street to show my best friend.

It was never connected to marriage. It was all about what the dress brought out in me. I became sacred, royal, elevated within the gown. Through wearing it, the power of ritual and symbolism tied to the dress became mine! It lifted me out of the ordinary, restrictive role I was assigned to perform. The gown uncovered the divine that I am.

I'm still mildly obsessed with dramatic dresses. But instead of separating them off for special occasions, I see every day as a worthy ritual. I am alive. I am here and I am sacred in my BE-ing. I dress as the divine femme every day, whatever that means for the day. This is not something to be saved or put off. I am now.

Here the flowers and veil represent mental, spiritual and psychological integration and ascension within. The lizard shows the fragility of life resting on the edge of the finger, but also the importance of all life and action no matter how small or seemingly fragile. The bride's fingers are crossed for hope as they look out at the landscape of light and dark shadows across their path cast by the trees. In the distance, the river flows.

This bride is not marrying anyone. They own their sacred power and the reality of the life they are living.

LIFE IS RITUAL

LIZARD BRIDE ONE
Acrylic on Masonite
32"x43" – 1998 | San Francisco, CA

Month: _____   Year: _____

Every time I engage my calendar, I am healing.

LIFE IS RITUAL

MONDAY

TUESDAY

WEDNESDAY

THURSDAY

FRIDAY

SATURDAY

SUNDAY

All
healing
counts
no matter
how small.

MONDAY

TUESDAY

WEDNESDAY

THURSDAY

FRIDAY

SATURDAY

SUNDAY

Life is ritual. My living is my healing.

MONDAY

TUESDAY

WEDNESDAY

THURSDAY

FRIDAY

SATURDAY

SUNDAY

maya 2008

I
am
OM

MONDAY

TUESDAY

WEDNESDAY

THURSDAY

FRIDAY

SATURDAY

SUNDAY

I am a part of the cosmic creative flow of the universe even if I don't know it or understand it.

LIFE IS RITUAL

MONDAY

TUESDAY

WEDNESDAY

THURSDAY

FRIDAY

SATURDAY

SUNDAY

2

EVERYTHING HEALS
Being present
with fear

*F*ear used to be a huge part of my life. It rattled my bones and sent my mind spinning. It was rooted deep in my childhood, so it would render my heart as useless as a mad cat. Hair raised, eyes wide, hissing and screeching at ghosts. I spent years healing fear. Clearing the fog that held the ghosts.

Now when fear comes up, instead of it clouding everything, it stands out. Singular. I can see it for what it is, navigate its familiar arch and receive its wisdom. It's a quick trip with a strong heart. But I only got strong by sitting with fear; by letting it rise and witnessing my reaction. I had to become familiar with my own fear to trust it as my teacher.

And fear taught me to trust my strong body. My body can hold me through the fear…I watched my body until I witnessed the rattling slow down and down into a low hum of pure being. Presence.

The central focus of this painting is the rattlesnake. I grew up hearing tales of how my one parent had to sweep the rattlesnakes off the back porch to go outside. Their stories terrified and fascinated me as a child. So, I familiarized myself with my fear by imagining a rattlesnake in my lap, akin to the Appalachian Christians who handle poisonous snakes.

I imagined what it would feel like to sit with a rattlesnake and not be afraid. I watched the fear in my body rise and rise until finally it peaked and began to rest down. I spent years witnessing my fear rest down until finally it stayed rested. I still have this artwork. It was up in my home for many years reminding me of my strong body.

WOMAN WITH RATTLESNAKE
Watercolor on Paper
26"x31" – 1996 | San Francisco, CA

Month: _____ Year: _____

Everything I do heals me, and I heal everything.

MONDAY

TUESDAY

WEDNESDAY

THURSDAY

FRIDAY

SATURDAY

SUNDAY

I witness
my fear
rise
knowing
that it will
rest back
down.

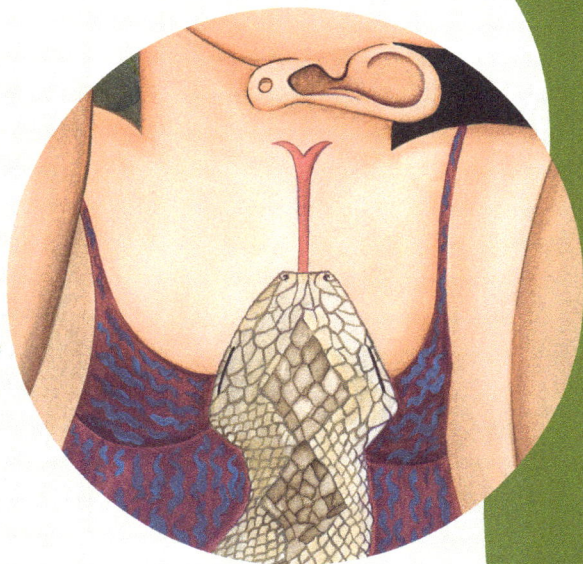

EVERYTHING HEALS

MONDAY

TUESDAY

WEDNESDAY

THURSDAY

FRIDAY

SATURDAY

SUNDAY

I acknowledge my fear. I witness how my body is strong enough for fear to pass through.

MONDAY

TUESDAY

WEDNESDAY

THURSDAY

FRIDAY

SATURDAY

SUNDAY

All that Is had to let go.

maya
2008

All that is had to let go.

MONDAY

TUESDAY

WEDNESDAY

THURSDAY

FRIDAY

SATURDAY

SUNDAY

I know that I can meet myself and my feelings and find my way. My spirit is strong, and healing is mine.

EVERYTHING HEALS

MONDAY

TUESDAY

WEDNESDAY

THURSDAY

FRIDAY

SATURDAY

SUNDAY

3.

CREATIVE SURRENDER
Sourcing courage
to act

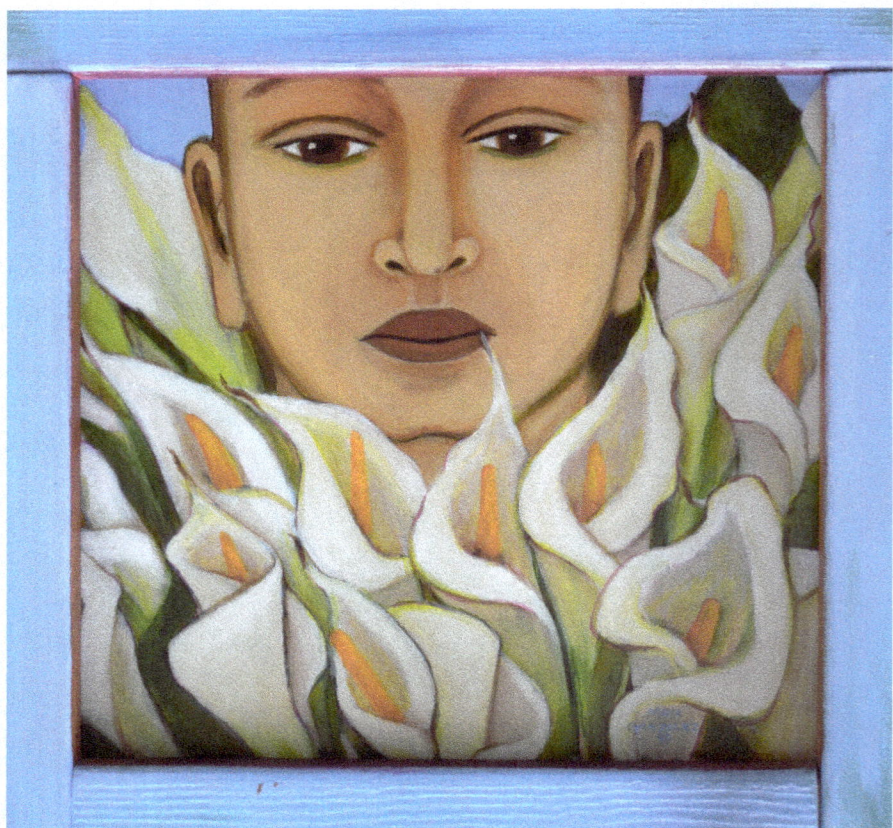

This piece began on a very large board with a jaguar and another person included. I worked on it and worked on it, but it refused to come together. Finally, I surrendered. There was only one small part that was working.

I pulled out my saw and cut off everything else.

I was right to trust myself. Freed, the small bit I saved held all the power of the larger piece.

I stared at that painting for years receiving its lesson. Not just trusting to free it from the rest of the board but understanding what was left and why it felt important to free… the unwinding of the blossoms, the piercing gaze amidst sturdy flowers, the sense of self rising from within.

It's the only time I've taken a saw to a painting.

Creativity can feel drastic or even destructive at times but trusting the process has always served me. At the beginning, I could not have predicted where things would go. I could not have known the freedom until I was brave enough to cut away everything that wasn't working.

Through my art I learn about myself and how to live. I am art. Life is art.

WOMAN WITH LILIES
Acrylic on Masonite
11"x11" – 1997 | San Francisco, CA

Month: Year:

Every time I engage my calendar, I am healing.

CREATIVE SURRENDER

MONDAY

TUESDAY

WEDNESDAY

THURSDAY

FRIDAY

SATURDAY

SUNDAY

I am naturally unfolding into my full self with the ease and grace of a lily.

MONDAY

TUESDAY

WEDNESDAY

THURSDAY

FRIDAY

SATURDAY

SUNDAY

As above so below. I let go and flow with the creative force of the cosmos.

MONDAY

TUESDAY

WEDNESDAY

THURSDAY

FRIDAY

SATURDAY

SUNDAY

I let
go of
attachments
and stay
open to what
works best.

MONDAY

TUESDAY

WEDNESDAY

THURSDAY

FRIDAY

SATURDAY

SUNDAY

46

I see through what's not working into the heart of a solution. I trust that I will know what to do when the time is right.

CREATIVE SURRENDER

MONDAY

TUESDAY

WEDNESDAY

THURSDAY

FRIDAY

SATURDAY

SUNDAY

4.

NEVER ALONE
Everything family

I Dance for My Tree
Acrylic on Masonite
20"x16" – 1998 | San Francisco, CA

I lived in a yurt in the deep woods of Oregon for 3 years. It was cold and dark in the winter and hot and bright in the summer but *way more*. The yurt was a half mile walk into the forest. I was one thin wall away from living in the brilliant and wild outside.

My art studio was a half hour away in town and I often got back to my yurt after dark.

I tried to prepare for the dark, but for some reason, no matter how many flashlights I bought, they all stopped working when I got to the land. I finally stopped buying them.

There were no lights to turn on until I got to my yurt. Just a ¼ mile of the crunching gravel path to remind me that my feet were on the right track, and I was not veering off into acres upon acres of black trees.

Instead of looking down or out, I learned to read the sky. It showed me the open path between the black trees. Certain ones guided me to turn here, go steady there, step up, step down. I counted on them in the dark. The trees were my friends.

In the painting, there is no inside or outside, just the inner self dancing with their guide.

Month: _____   Year: _____

Everything I do heals me, and I heal everything.

4

NEVER ALONE

53

MONDAY

TUESDAY

WEDNESDAY

THURSDAY

FRIDAY

SATURDAY

SUNDAY

I am tree
dancing.
I reach
and
I rise.

MONDAY

TUESDAY

WEDNESDAY

THURSDAY

FRIDAY

SATURDAY

SUNDAY

I feel
the tree
that I am.
A solid
trunk.
A firm
hold on
earth.

NEVER ALONE

MONDAY

TUESDAY

WEDNESDAY

THURSDAY

FRIDAY

SATURDAY

SUNDAY

I am the bird
singing the
song. I am the
tree touching
the sky. I heal
everything
because I am
everything.

MONDAY

TUESDAY

WEDNESDAY

THURSDAY

FRIDAY

SATURDAY

SUNDAY

I let go
into the
power of
my own
nature.

MONDAY

TUESDAY

WEDNESDAY

THURSDAY

FRIDAY

SATURDAY

SUNDAY

5

RIGHT RELATIONSHIP

Dancing away from judgment and sacrifice

I grew up in the Mojave Desert. Rattlesnakes were a thing. We didn't have to sweep them off the porch to go outside, but they were around once you got out of town. You had to be aware. I remember once my parent got out a small box, the kind rosaries are usually in. They lifted the cover to show me their precious collection of rattles. I was allowed to touch them, and they rattled as they flopped from side to side, perfect symmetry for the shake. My parent worked outside the city limit at times and rattlesnakes would cross their path.

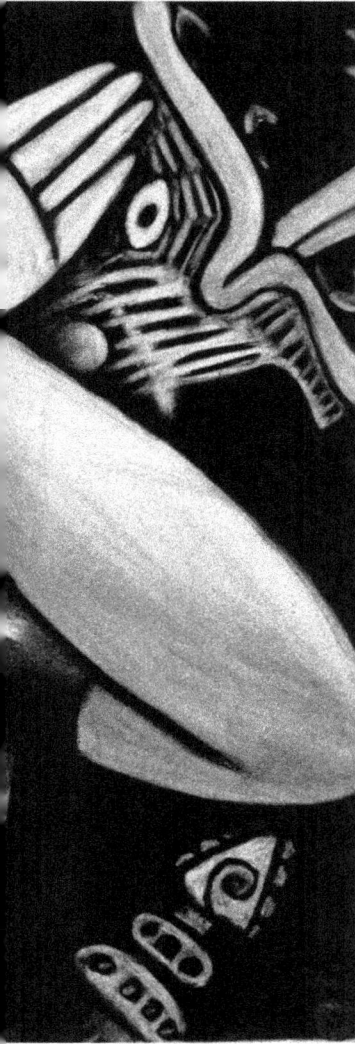

They would smash the head with a big rock then cut off the rattle. At the time, I thought this was brave and right. And they got a prize for their courage.

When I got a little older, I learned about the massive rattlesnake massacres they used to have in the desert. Men would drive the rattlesnakes from their dens and *kill them all*. Older still, I learned how rattlesnakes were highly revered and used in ritual sacrifice in Mesoamerica. Feared or revered, everywhere a dead snake. Of course, all this sat next to what I had been taught about the snake who tempted Eve.

When my family disowned me because of their queerphobia, the snake became a deeply personal symbol. Initially, the snake was nature, fear, danger, power. But eventually, the snake meant projection, sacrifice, discernment.

The idea of UNsacrificing the snake rose in me. This means owning one's projections and fear in the face of nature. There is nothing inherently evil or worthy of sacrifice about any living being. All life is valuable and sacred. One's fear doesn't negate that. Here, instead of using the stick to drive the snakes from their dens, the stick is conscious and is being waved over the heart to drive out projections and fear. There is a feather in the other hand to reference Quetzalcoatl, the plumed and sacred serpent of Mesoamerica.

RIGHT RELATIONSHIP

Month: Year:

Every time I engage my calendar, I am healing.

RIGHT RELATIONSHIP

MONDAY

TUESDAY

WEDNESDAY

THURSDAY

FRIDAY

SATURDAY

SUNDAY

All
life is
valuable.
All life
is sacred.

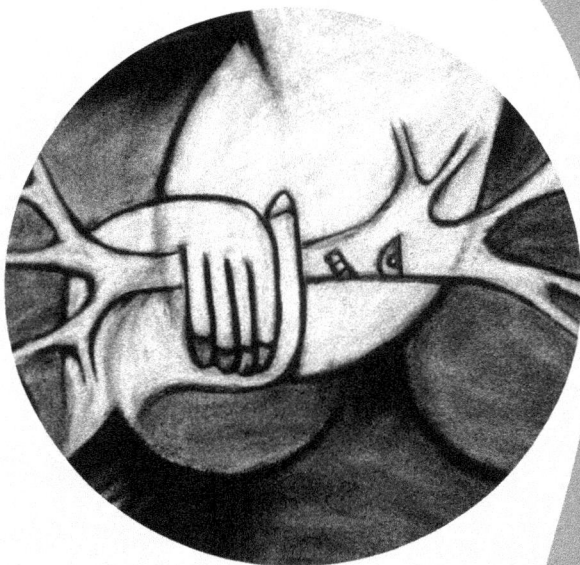

MONDAY

TUESDAY

WEDNESDAY

THURSDAY

FRIDAY

SATURDAY

SUNDAY

I am the
snake and
the snake is
me. I hug the
earth freely.

MONDAY

TUESDAY

WEDNESDAY

THURSDAY

FRIDAY

SATURDAY

SUNDAY

maya 2008 YUBA

The power of nature flows through
my being. I am free to be.

MONDAY

TUESDAY

WEDNESDAY

THURSDAY

FRIDAY

SATURDAY

SUNDAY

I relax into my own flow.
I belong here.

MONDAY

TUESDAY

WEDNESDAY

THURSDAY

FRIDAY

SATURDAY

SUNDAY

FULLY PRESENT
Finding balance within

6

*F*or years, this piece hung above the kitchen sink where I used to live. I spent hours doing dishes under its massive glow. Then it was stored in my art studio for 15 years. Until I had it back up in my home, I didn't know how much I needed this painting.

I paint to integrate. It's a ritual that engages me physically, emotionally, psychologically and spiritually. The symbology of this piece gathers me together and keeps me strong. At the heart is the pomegranate. It always represents the fragility and complexity of life. I must be patient to extract the healing juice.

The person in the painting is riding a tobacco leaf, connecting them to the spiritual journey. The dots and symbols embedded on the leaf represent guides and remind me that although it may seem ephemeral, there is always spiritual support that can carry me.

Spiritual connection is echoed in the ring of fire above where there are 13 Mesoamerican symbols of the eye. A traditional crown hovers over the head of the super strong, fully embodied femme in a birthing position.

The fire represents expanding the mind into bigger more spiritually focused consciousness and the crown signifies divinity and access. It ties the person to their precolonial past and other ways of thinking and being. The imagery is laid out like an altar with circles throughout. The physical is centered, but it is held in place by the spiritual journey and expanded consciousness above and below.

Just writing out the symbology deepens my experience of the painting. I'm sitting beside it as I write this. Total, holistic power. Everything heals. Every momeant. Now.

KING AND THE COUNCIL
Acrylic on Masonite
36"x48" – 1997 | San Francisco, CA

Month: Year:

Everything I do heals me, and I heal everything.

FULLY PRESENT

MONDAY

TUESDAY

WEDNESDAY

THURSDAY

FRIDAY

SATURDAY

SUNDAY

The juice is precious. Be patient.

MONDAY

TUESDAY

WEDNESDAY

THURSDAY

FRIDAY

SATURDAY

SUNDAY

I balance.
I am body
and spirit.
I balance.

MONDAY

TUESDAY

WEDNESDAY

THURSDAY

FRIDAY

SATURDAY

SUNDAY

FULLY PRESENT

The song
of me
vibrates
throughout
the cosmos.

MONDAY

TUESDAY

WEDNESDAY

THURSDAY

FRIDAY

SATURDAY

SUNDAY

My divine ancestors exist within me. My existence rides on their ritual and song.

MONDAY

TUESDAY

WEDNESDAY

THURSDAY

FRIDAY

SATURDAY

SUNDAY

7.

UP UP UP
Expansion and elevation

*W*hen I healed from heavy metals in 2006, everything I knew changed. I lost nearly all the people I considered family... again, my work got smaller and smaller and more stylized, my world got bigger, my body wanted to dance all the time, and I found love.

I remember it was weird. Having had lots of strong spiritual and physical experiences I can say very clearly, healing feels weird. Bringing in greater love and awareness and letting go of the past can really rearrange one. It feels free but it can blow circuits out and create profoundly dramatic scenarios to help one's path shift.

Maturing also feels weird. It used to surprise me when I would find myself letting go and just relaxing down into being me, deepening into who I always knew I was. It's glorious, but it's also weird. Maybe disorienting would be a better word. Maybe. Becoming your full self takes adjusting.

I am more familiar with the dance now. I have healed and healed again. I know I can.

I know I have to lean into the rhythm and trust that I am built for this no matter what comes.

In this small drawing, the person is beginning to dance the bigger dance. The first moves may look and feel weird and awkward. It suddenly feels like another eye and layers of wings have sprouted! But the need, the drive to let go into the dance is an important part of healing.

I freely dance into my weirdest self. This heals me.

UP UP UP

THREE WING WOMAN
Pen and Colored Pencil on Archival Paper
4 ½" x 6 ½" – 2010 | San Francisco, CA

Month: _____   Year: _____

UP UP UP

MONDAY

TUESDAY

WEDNESDAY

THURSDAY

FRIDAY

SATURDAY

SUNDAY

It's ok to
feel weird
through
healing.
I naturally
adjust.

UP UP UP

MONDAY

TUESDAY

WEDNESDAY

THURSDAY

FRIDAY

SATURDAY

SUNDAY

Every day
I take a
momeant to
be with my
thoughts,
my feelings.
I know my
current self.

UP UP UP

MONDAY

TUESDAY

WEDNESDAY

THURSDAY

FRIDAY

SATURDAY

SUNDAY

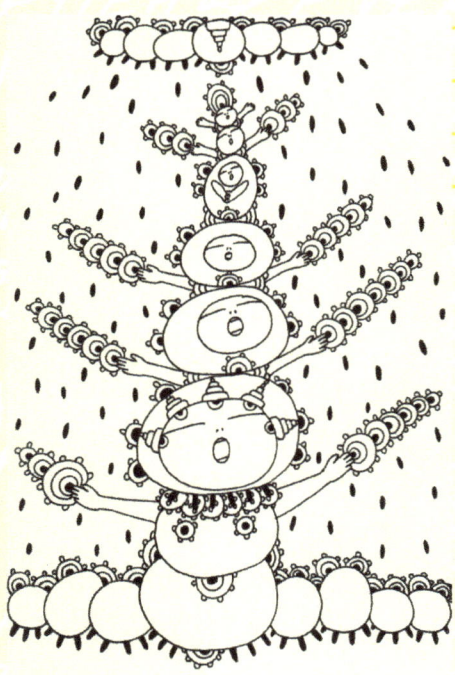

love.maya '08

UP UP UP

I look up
to the sky
and sing and
rattle and
receive the
rain. I am here
to grow.

MONDAY

TUESDAY

WEDNESDAY

THURSDAY

FRIDAY

SATURDAY

SUNDAY

I allow all of myself to be here now.

UP UP UP

7.

MONDAY

TUESDAY

WEDNESDAY

THURSDAY

FRIDAY

SATURDAY

SUNDAY

104

CORE BEING
Deep roots of peace

8

I didn't know I got to have peace. I grew up thinking peace was something you had to fight for, something outside of yourself, something nice and beautiful, maybe in the future…

Until I engaged peace, I didn't know that peace is my core self and that I can tap into it at any time. I realized that I must be in relationship with peace. I must know peace to imagine a peaceful world, let alone know peace within myself. And peace, like everything, is not what I thought it was. It's not soft and fluffy or smooth and easy. It's all the many ways peace needs to be. Peace is gritty and sad sometimes. It's still peace.

I learned that it's not about hating war, but loving peace. And if I am peace at my core, then it's also about loving that peace within myself. Where I used to meditate on world peace…*War coming to an end…* Now I meditate on inner peace. I imagine all of us deeply loving the peace within and acting from that place.

There is so much peace to heal within, but to clear my path, I had to relearn who I am. I had to negotiate that I am not who I was told or taught I am. I am free. I am something altogether different at core.

This is a very small piece, but I like to imagine it huge. Larger than life. I am resting in front of it and filling my thoughts, my body, my heart with peace. Peace is rooting in every cell. Peace inside. Peace outside. I use flowers to symbolize peace in honor of Allen Ginsberg and the peace movement of the 60's. Every time I see a flower I think of peace.

Now. I am the flower. I am peace. Inside and out. Peace begins with me. I begin within. I commit to peace.

CORE BEING

FLOWER SOUL COMMUNION
Pen and Colored Pencil on Archival Paper
4 ½" x 6 ½" – 2010 | San Francisco, CA

Month: Year:

Everything I do heals me, and I heal everything.

MONDAY

TUESDAY

WEDNESDAY

THURSDAY

FRIDAY

SATURDAY

SUNDAY

Peace is
blooming
in me.

MONDAY

TUESDAY

WEDNESDAY

THURSDAY

FRIDAY

SATURDAY

SUNDAY

My
inner peace
expands
until I see
it all
around
me.

MONDAY

TUESDAY

WEDNESDAY

THURSDAY

FRIDAY

SATURDAY

SUNDAY

My song is strong. My peace branches out in all directions from deep within.

MONDAY

TUESDAY

WEDNESDAY

THURSDAY

FRIDAY

SATURDAY

SUNDAY

My deep inner peace builds me up, makes me stable and opens my mind.

MONDAY

TUESDAY

WEDNESDAY

THURSDAY

FRIDAY

SATURDAY

SUNDAY

9

ELEPHANT SIZE
Strength and love

STRONG LOVE ELEPHANT
Pen and Watercolor on Archival Paper
5 ¼" x 4 ⅞" – 2010 | San Francisco, CA

*C*urrently the elephant is the largest land animal alive. When I was in India, I saw one being groomed on a side street. They were heavily painted and decorated with ornaments and cloth. I don't imagine they liked any of that or being on a street in a crowded city or being what? Domesticated? Enslaved? What's the right word?

Being close to them I could sense the power just in their size alone. Massive. Technically, they could do anything they wanted—if they wanted to.

This is not a painting of a real elephant. Real elephants should be unencumbered and free. This elephant is a symbol for the big truths, including the big self.

I am much bigger than I have been traditionally taught and trained.

I am body, mind, heart, spirit and the unknown.

I am elephant.

I am love.

I am enormous.

I am free to be my biggest self.

Month: _____   Year: _____

Every time I engage my calendar, I am healing.

9

ELEPHANT SIZE

MONDAY

TUESDAY

WEDNESDAY

THURSDAY

FRIDAY

SATURDAY

SUNDAY

I decorate myself with love because I am love. I can see my BIG self.

MONDAY

TUESDAY

WEDNESDAY

THURSDAY

FRIDAY

SATURDAY

SUNDAY

My BIG self carries and cares for me. I am never alone.

ELEPHANT SIZE

MONDAY

TUESDAY

WEDNESDAY

THURSDAY

FRIDAY

SATURDAY

SUNDAY

maya 2008

My own
song
propels
me higher
and higher.

MONDAY

TUESDAY

WEDNESDAY

THURSDAY

FRIDAY

SATURDAY

SUNDAY

Love surrounds me inside and out.

MONDAY

TUESDAY

WEDNESDAY

THURSDAY

FRIDAY

SATURDAY

SUNDAY

10

NOURISHMEANT
Everything sacred

arias '98

*E*ating has been a constant lesson for me. I taught myself how to bake as a kid. I loved the tools and alchemy, the smells, the nuance of recipes and flavors. Cookies and pies were my specialty. The more rustic and homemade-y the better. Woven crusts, homegrown rhubarb, meringue peaks, angel food cake!

It wasn't until I was in my 30's that I figured out I had serious gluten sensitivities. After crying a couple of times, I learned how to bake gluten free. Not a problem. I loved rice and I learned its secrets.

Then over a few years I started having more and more arthritis symptoms, just like one of my grandparents. As a child, I watched their crocheting fall as their fingers bent and twisted away. So, I adjusted my baking again and learned to let go of all grains and sugar.

Then I got cancer. Really? My lesson with food isn't over. I'm learning all over again. I thought I knew something. But I found out I know nothing. Again.

What I do know is food is life. Food is love.

Here the person is in a prayerful state. It looks like they're about to eat a grape, but the context shows it's much more than that. The veil and single grape echo communion in church. They are communing with the grape.

Food is sacred.

Food heals.

NOURISHMEANT

EVERYTHING A SACRAMENT
Acrylic on Masonite
16" x 22" – 1998 | San Francisco, CA

Month: Year:

Everything I do heals me, and I heal everything.

NOURISHMEANT

MONDAY

TUESDAY

WEDNESDAY

THURSDAY

FRIDAY

SATURDAY

SUNDAY

I take a
momeant
to
commune.

MONDAY

TUESDAY

WEDNESDAY

THURSDAY

FRIDAY

SATURDAY

SUNDAY

The sacredness within me connects with the sacredness of what I eat.

MONDAY

TUESDAY

WEDNESDAY

THURSDAY

FRIDAY

SATURDAY

SUNDAY

I hear the
song of
the fruit
growing.

maya '08

MONDAY

TUESDAY

WEDNESDAY

THURSDAY

FRIDAY

SATURDAY

SUNDAY

144

What I eat feeds my soul.

MONDAY

TUESDAY

WEDNESDAY

THURSDAY

FRIDAY

SATURDAY

SUNDAY

146

11

ONE ONENESS
Everything conscious

This piece is one of the first paintings I did once I realized how to be an artist, or how to use art to heal myself and express something beyond the physical realm. It's a long story that I won't tell here. I'll just say that I learned not to think, but to listen when I paint.

Often, I don't understand my work fully until many years later. As I draw or paint, I allow my intuition to tap into the connections on a deep spiritual level. I pray or meditate into my work as I create it and constantly remove judgment to keep it flowing. If something gets jammed up in the process, I put it down for a moment and allow things to adjust within myself until it feels open again. I keep an eye on the spiritual as well as the physical realm. This keeps me in the flow and in right relationship with the creative force.

I never feel like I'm blocked. Even when I pause, it is part of the greater flow.

Here the fern is perceiving the deeper truth of spiritual reality and interconnectedness, including the person. From the solely physical perspective however, it may just look like a person standing next to a plant.

I call in a huge shift in consciousness. There is so much to learn beyond what I have been taught about everything. Radically playing with my perspective, opening to creative interpretations and symbols expands my mind. I reconnect with the consciousness of nature all around me. And wonder, how is nature perceiving me?

ONE ONENESS

WHEN FERNS DREAM
Watercolor on Archival Paper
9" x 12" – circa 1990 | Eugene, OR

149

Month: Year:

150

ONE ONENESS

MONDAY

TUESDAY

WEDNESDAY

THURSDAY

FRIDAY

SATURDAY

SUNDAY

I am part of all that is. I am dreaming it as it is dreaming me.

MONDAY

TUESDAY

WEDNESDAY

THURSDAY

FRIDAY

SATURDAY

SUNDAY

I call myself
in from all
directions.
I am centered
in this perfect
moment where
I belong.

ONE ONENESS

155

MONDAY

TUESDAY

WEDNESDAY

THURSDAY

FRIDAY

SATURDAY

SUNDAY

156

I hear
the song
within all
things.

MONDAY

TUESDAY

WEDNESDAY

THURSDAY

FRIDAY

SATURDAY

SUNDAY

I am
connecting
on deeper
and deeper
levels with
the reality
of nature.

MONDAY

TUESDAY

WEDNESDAY

THURSDAY

FRIDAY

SATURDAY

SUNDAY

12

UNVEILED
Burning away illusion

Ecstasy Burning Through (Woman with Black Veil)
Acrylic on Masonite
22" x 17 ½" – 1997 | San Francisco, CA

*F*rom claiming the divine femme to reconnecting with nature, I have spent my life gathering the tools to create a foundation of inner strength.

It has been essential to see through the illusions, the superficiality and judgment the world has tried to place on me and everything around me. I have learned that no matter what is going on I must be able to see the real me and my own divine nature to be whole.

Without illusion, I have become more conscious of the present and my power in it. Every moment I see.

Here a person is lifting the veil so that their strong heart can burn it away. The veil is based on one my parent wore to church when I was a young child. I wore a white one. I loved the drama of it but understood little more, only that women and girls were supposed to wear them to church. It was tradition. Covering ourselves meant we were good. Veils represent illusion and feature prominently in my work. A big part of my healing has been seeing through what has been placed on me.

I have learned,

the stronger the heart the weaker the illusion.

Month: **Year:**

UNVEILED

MONDAY

TUESDAY

WEDNESDAY

THURSDAY

FRIDAY

SATURDAY

SUNDAY

I
am free
to be
exactly
who I am.

MONDAY

TUESDAY

WEDNESDAY

THURSDAY

FRIDAY

SATURDAY

SUNDAY

My connection to the divine femme is unquestionable because I am a part of all that is.

MONDAY

TUESDAY

WEDNESDAY

THURSDAY

FRIDAY

SATURDAY

SUNDAY

I form my physical environment.

I create. Therefore I am.

MAY

2008

MONDAY

TUESDAY

WEDNESDAY

THURSDAY

FRIDAY

SATURDAY

SUNDAY

I am a freely flowing force of nature.

MONDAY

TUESDAY

WEDNESDAY

THURSDAY

FRIDAY

SATURDAY

SUNDAY

174

13

SYN*THE*SIS
Transforming through healing

and actually fight with this Phi·lis'- tine." 33 But Saul said to David: "You are not able to go against this Phi·lis'tine to fight with him, for you are but a boy, and he is a man of war from his boyhood." 34 And David went on to say to Saul: "Your servant became a shepherd of his father among the flock, and there came a lion, and also a bear, and [each] carried off a sheep from the drove. 35 And I went out after it and struck it down and made the rescue from its mouth. When it began rising against me, I grabbed hold of its beard and struck it down and put it to death. 36 Both the lion and the bear your servant struck down, and this uncircumcised Phi·lis'tine must become like one of them, for he has taunted the battle lines of the living God." 37 Then David added: "Jehovah, who delivered me from the paw of the lion and from the paw of the bear, he it is who will deliver me from the hand of this Phi·lis'tine." At this Saul said to David: "Go, and may Jehovah himself prove to be with you."

38 Saul now went clothing David with his garments, and he put a copper helmet upon his head, after which he clothed him with a coat of mail. 39 Then David girded his sword on over his garments and undertook to go, but he could not, because he had not tried them out. Finally David said to Saul: "I am unable to go in these things, for I have not tried them out." So David removed them off him. 40 And he proceeded to take his staff in his hand and to choose for himself the five smoothest stones from the torrent valley and to place them in his shepherds' bag that served him as a receptacle, and in his hand was his sling. And he began approaching the Phi·lis'tine.

41 And the Phi·lis'tine began to come, coming nearer and nearer to David, and the man carrying the large shield was ahead of him. 42 Now when the Phi·lis'tine

looked and saw David, he began despising him because he proved to be a boy and ruddy, and of beautiful appearance. 43 So the Phi·lis'tine said to David: "Am I a dog, so that you are coming to me with staves?" With that the Phi·lis'tine called down evil upon David by his gods. 44 And the Phi·lis'tine went on to say to David: "Just come to me, and I will give your flesh to the fowls of the heavens and to the beasts of the field."

45 In turn David said to the Phi·lis'tine: "You are coming to me with a sword and with a spear and with a javelin, but I am coming to you with the name of Jehovah of armies, the God of the battle lines of Israel, whom you have taunted. 46 This day Jehovah will surrender you into my hand, and I shall certainly strike you down and remove your head off you; and I shall certainly give the carcasses of the camp of the Phi·lis'tines this day to the fowls of the heavens and to the wild beasts of the earth; and people of all the earth will know that there exists a God belonging to Israel. 47 And all this congregation will know that neither with sword nor with spear does Jehovah save, because to Jehovah belongs the battle, and he must give you men into our hand."

48 And it occurred that the Phi·lis'tine rose and kept coming and drawing nearer to meet David, and David began hurrying and running toward the battle line to meet the Phi·lis'tine. 49 Then David thrust his hand into his bag and took from there a stone and slung it, so that he struck the Phi·lis'tine in his forehead and the stone sank into his forehead, and he went falling upon his face to the earth. 50 So David, with a sling and a stone, proved stronger than the Phi·lis'tine and struck the Phi·lis'tine down and put him to death; and there was no sword in David's hand. 51 And David kept running and got to stand over the Phi·lis'tine. The

When the heavy metal poisoning had me too weak to paint, I began using ink on vintage book pages. It was the most gentle, easy form of expression I could find. The page was so fragile, and the ink was so strong. The art just fell out of me.

I was met with Hello Kitty and Snow White, some dwarves and so many rabbits and snakes. Bambi was there and Holly Hobbie too. And they were all dancing through the painted books of my ancient ancestors, the Mesoamerican codices showing ritual, sacrifice and the passage of time. Oh my!

The imagery spoke to me. But sometimes I could not say how. I lived with the lead and the arsenic, the cadmium and the mercury wrangling my nerves and sending my spirit soaring into the cosmos. Out there somewhere, I was held. I was healed.

JaguarKitty is one of my favorite pieces from that time. Today it reminds me that I can heal anything. Something I didn't know then. No matter how scary, no matter how confusing, there is a way. Keep flowing.

In the corner you can see the symbol for arsenic and time spent sick. JaguarKitty is a synthesis of my innocence and my power, my spirit and my physical, my truth beyond the illusion.

I am.

One with all.

SYN*THE*SIS

JaguarKitty
Pen and Ink on Bible Page (Samuel 17:33-5)
4 ½" x 6 ½" – 2003 | San Francisco, CA

Month: Year:

SYN*THE*SIS

MONDAY

TUESDAY

WEDNESDAY

THURSDAY

FRIDAY

SATURDAY

SUNDAY

I am a
synthesis of
all healing
within me—
past, present
and future.

MONDAY

TUESDAY

WEDNESDAY

THURSDAY

FRIDAY

SATURDAY

SUNDAY

Every part of me is healing all the time.

MONDAY

TUESDAY

WEDNESDAY

THURSDAY

FRIDAY

SATURDAY

SUNDAY

I heal
everything
inside and
out.

MONDAY

TUESDAY

WEDNESDAY

THURSDAY

FRIDAY

SATURDAY

SUNDAY

I
am wild
and free.

SYN*THE*SIS

MONDAY

TUESDAY

WEDNESDAY

THURSDAY

FRIDAY

SATURDAY

SUNDAY

HEAL
EVERYTHING
EVERYTHING
HEALS

TIME TO HEAL

NOW